A Goat Named Josephine

Lessons From the Barnyard Vol. 1

Emma Byers

Copyright © 2017 Emma Byers

All rights reserved.

ISBN-10: 1540837262
ISBN-13: 978-1540837264

DEDICATION

To Rhonda,

A surprise blessing in my life; a special sister in Christ, and with whom my goat shenanigans began. I am so thankful that God brought you into my life, for all of the advice, laughs, encouragement and help that you bring me.

CONTENTS

	Acknowledgments	i
1	A Name With Meaning	3
2	Do Goats Eat Everything?	Pg 8
3	Enough Food For Each Day	Pg 15
4	A Shelter From The Storm	Pg 19
	Pictures	Pgs 26-29
5	Pedicures	Pg 30
6	Man Makes Plans…	Pg 34
7	A Believer Believes	Pg 37
8	Isolation	Pg 42
9	My Way Or His Way?	Pg 51
	A Note From The Author	Pg 55

ACKNOWLEDGMENTS

I want to thank my husband, Daniel, for always going along with what I believe that God has told me to do. The instructions do not always make sense, but you always support me and help me to fulfill His plans and purposes in my life. I love you.

1

A Name With Meaning

Josephine. What a weird name for a goat. She's not a Dolly, Molly, Maggie or Goatie; Josephine is the name I gave her when she came to live on our humble Circle 4B Ranch in "small town," Texas. A birthday present from my mother, who is the coolest mother ever to give a goat as a present, I knew that she needed a name that had meaning. A name that stood for something, a declaration if you will, of who she was to me.

When I met Josephine, she was underweight, recovering from a bout with worms, and was not real pretty to behold. Her dull, drab, brown colored coat was frazzled and coarse, her white frosted ears were droopy, her eyes were dull and lightless, but it was her eyes that captivated me. She looked at me with her amber colored eyes and she seemed to look right through me, to the depths of who I was. She didn't just look at me, she studied me. She watched my every move with her head tilted to the side, like she was trying to take it all in.

My husband was skeptical on bringing her home because of the way she looked, but I knew she was to be ours. We had moved out into the country on 40 acres a few months before, and from that moment, visions of animals danced in my head. As we strived to make it the ranch of all of our dreams, I had a desire to have farm fresh milk for my house. Knowing that we didn't need 2-3 gallons of milk a day, a cow was out of my thinking, but a dairy goat could work. I set myself to research what kind of dairy goat and what properties of milk I wanted, and how much milk I thought we would use.

I quickly narrowed my list to a Nubian or an Alpine, both of which should give over a half a gallon a day. I watched Craigslist, searched websites, and checked feed store ads before finally posting in a local group on Facebook as to what I was looking for. A lady contacted me saying she had a Nubian/Alpine cross that had a baby on her side that she would sell pretty cheap.

That is how I met Josephine. I can't remember if the lady who had her had a name for her, but as we were trailering her and her baby home, I began to search for a name.

We had been on the ranch for a few months, and had not secured employment in our new town. We were living by faith on what we thought God had opened a door to when we moved. We were surviving on savings and retirement money, and were ready for God to open the next door. We were ready for increase financially, and I was ready for animal increase.

It seemed only right when I searched for names that meant, "increase." It was my way to laugh in the devil's face; to declare that we would increase regardless of what our circumstances looked like in the natural, because we believed God. The name would be a reminder and a faith statement every time I called it. It wasn't just a name. It was my faith out loud!

Josephine. "God Will Increase." More than a name; it was a promise. A promise from God Himself.

"Now it shall come to pass, if you diligently obey the voice of the Lord your God, to observe carefully all His commandments which I command you today, that the Lord your God will set you high above all nations of the earth. And all these blessings shall come upon you and

overtake you, because you obey the voice of the Lord your God: 'Blessed shall you be in the city, and blessed shall you be in the country. Blessed shall be the fruit of your body, the produce of your ground and the increase of your herds, the increase of your cattle and the offspring of your flocks'".
Deuteronomy 28:1-4

We brought home a scruffy looking goat that had a promise hidden in her new name and dared to declare that God said He would bless her and increase her, and our herds. Two goats; not quite a herd, but little did I know, it was a start to something more than I could have imagined.

We got to work putting the nutrition in her that her body needed, and she didn't seem to mind all of the extra yummy things that she was receiving. We brushed her, fed her, loved on her, and not before too long, a bright, shiny copper colored coat started to emerge. Finally after all that dull, drab brown colored coat was replaced with new hair, spots began to emerge, and when all was said and done, Josephine looked like a new goat! She was shiny and soft, and spotted to my amazement. Her ears, although floppy, no longer drooped and there was a spring in her step. Where bumpy ribs had been before, soft flesh had covered the bones. God had increased.

I had no way of knowing that God would use this goat with humble beginnings, to teach me so many lessons about Him, living for Him and even about myself.

2

Do Goats Eat Everything?

I can vividly remember a cartoon that I saw as a child that featured a white billy goat with horns who ate anything and everything. Laundry hanging out on the line, all of the homeowner's flowers and shrubs, and every tin can he came in contact with, were his to be devoured. As an adult, I fell in with the majority of people who have been indoctrinated, even if only by cartoons, that teach that goats will eat everything at your house.

When I brought Josephine home, I put her in a pasture that had a barn and lots of green plants to graze on. Much to my surprise, she didn't like most of the those amazing green plants that were in her new pasture. She would walk through the tall grass, with her nose in the air, and nibble the tops of the plants that she deemed worthy. The hay that the cattle were more than happy to eat, she walked away from.

I started to read and research and learned that goats are picky! My old tires and rusty cans were definitely safe, but what would I feed this poor skinny goat? I learned that goats are browsers that prefer to eat the tops of the plants versus eating the plant down to the ground. The thought of just throwing her out into a pasture and not have to worry about feeding her, became a distant memory as I searched to find food that she would eat and that would cause her to flourish.

After a few weeks, I did get her food all figured out. She settled in with a sweet coastal hay and a grain supplement that would add in some vitamins and nutrients that she needed. I was more than surprised when God began to speak to me about the way Josephine ate. He pointed out that she didn't just gobble up everything that came her way, but that she sorted through what was fed to her as she took it in.

"Beloved, do not believe every spirit, but test the spirits, whether they are of God; because many false prophets have gone out into the world. By this you know the Spirit of God: Every spirit that confesses that Jesus Christ has come in the flesh is of God, and every spirit that does not confess that Jesus Christ has come in the flesh is not of God. And this is the spirit of the Antichrist, which you have heard was coming, and is now already in the world." 1 John 4:1-3

There are many times when we as Christians have a thought, hear a conversation, a message, or even a word spoken from a pulpit; and it sounds good to our human reasoning. We analyze it and try to fit it in to our lives and see if it will work for us, long before we check to see if it is biblical. Just because it comes from a news source, a pulpit, a friend, or a family member; does not mean that it is in the Bible, or is how a Christian should live.

Like Josephine, we need to test what we are about to gobble up and house on the inside of us. The things that we allow to go in to our ears and down to the foundations of what we believe had better be in line with God's Holy

Word, or we are headed for disaster, no matter how appealing it may seem to us in the natural.

A friend of mine whom I cherish deeply, had a YouTube video sent to her not that long ago, and it didn't set well with her. She asked if I would look at it and see what I thought/

The person in the video, had their own channel, a huge list of videos, and the audience that it showed as the person spoke was a very large one. I can tell you that, in less than five minutes into what they spoke on, I shut it off. It was not biblical. Just because someone has a large following, a big building, or some kind of degree or experience, does not mean that what is coming out of them is from God.

It is so important in the time that we are living in, to be in the Bible and to know what it says, so that when we are presented with something, we know if it is from God or not. There are only two options, something is either of God, or of the world which is under the sway of the devil.

"We know that we are of God, and the whole world lies under the sway of the wicked one. And we know that the Son of God has come and has given us an

understanding, that we may know Him who is true; and we are in Him who is true, in His Son Jesus Christ. This is the true God and eternal life." 1 John 5:19-20

Jesus did not leave us to endure this corruptible world alone! He came to bring life and truth, so that we can live with Him forever in eternity, but also so that we can take Him with us in our day to day life on earth. We don't leave the truth in the pews at church or on the pages of the Bible, we take it with us when we ingest it by feeding on it daily.

We feed on truth, pick out the weeds and spit them out from our mouths and minds. I have watched Josephine eat numerous times and I have seen her take a mouth full of grain, sort through it in her cheeks and let the pieces she didn't want fall from the corners of her mouth. It wasn't an accident, she purposely spit out the same circular piece of grain with every mouth full. She was sorting the good from the bad, and only ingesting the right grains.

God showed me that I need to be like her, to weed through the things that come at me and only take in what is right. To test everything, no matter the source, against the truth of the Bible, and spit out the things that don't test true. This ensures that we live and walk in the truth, but also that we are spreading only the truth to others. That we are not regurgitating anything that goes against God and His Holy Word to those around us.

A family member of mine had a medical diagnosis a while back that looked like it could be cancer. It was astonishing how many people would tell this person how they could "cure" the cancer that they had if they only: stopped eating sugar; went on a low-carb diet; started juicing every day; ate only organic food; and so on and so forth. People's ideas on the subject varied, but everyone whom my family member spoke with was sure they were giving them the cure to cancer.

Do not misunderstand me, I am not making fun of, or putting the benefits of any of these suggestions down. As for me, I believe that God sent Jesus to take our sicknesses and diseases, but I also believe that He gave us doctors and modern medicine to utilize them when we need them.

Each of the people that told my family member a cure, believed something based on what they had heard, or read, or saw. Did those suggestions hold up to modern medical science? I don't believe that I am qualified to make that decision, but I do believe, like everything, we need to test what we hear is presented as truth and decide for ourselves based on what we know about God.

3

Enough Food For Each Day

Josephine settled in and was happy with her new feeding regiment. She had blossomed into a beautiful, healthy girl with more personality than her body could hold. She was smart and inquisitive, and always had to be in the middle of anything going on. As I began to learn her and her quirks, I noticed that she never touched any hay that fell from her manger onto the ground.

That weird trait got me thinking about the children of Israel.

The children of Israel had suffered slavery for hundreds of years in Egypt before God sent Moses to lead His people to freedom. We all know the story of the events that surrounded Israel being set free, and their trek to the promised land. They had escaped the horrific conditions of slavery in Egypt, but ended up in a desert without food or water; yet, God had provisions for them. Every morning's dew brought manna, food for the whole nation without lack, and each person could collect whatever he thought he could eat for the day.

"So when they measured it by omers, he who gathered much had nothing left over, and he who gathered little had no lack. Every man had gathered according to each one's need. And Moses said, "Let no one leave any of it till morning." Notwithstanding they did not heed Moses. But some of them left part of it until morning, and it bred worms and stank. And Moses was angry with them. So they gathered it every morning, every man according to his need. And when the sun became hot, it melted." Exodus 16:18-21

Moses instructed the people to only gather as much manna as they needed for the day, and to not save any for the next day. If any manna was held for the next day, it spoiled and had to be thrown away.

Did you eat today? Was yesterday's food enough nourishment that you are not in need of calories today to sustain your body and refill your energy? Of course not! You woke up today and ingested food because that is what your body needs to be able to make it through the day.

We need to be feeding on the word of God every day! We cannot rely on our spiritual food from yesterday to sustain us today. I know life is busy, but it is necessary for victory over whatever may come your way, to be prepared, full of the word, and ready to expend it throughout your day.

"All Scripture is given by inspiration of God, and is profitable for doctrine, for reproof, for correction, for instruction in righteousness, that the man of God may be complete, thoroughly equipped for every good work." 2 Timothy 3:16-17

Josephine, wanted new hay not yesterday's leftovers. She wanted the fresh, sweet taste that comes from a newly opened flake of hay. As we open the word every day, we are surely to be met with something new

that we may have read a hundred times before,
but now see it in a new way.

4

A Shelter From the Storm

On our ranch, our first acquisitions were Angus beef cattle. These cattle were not what I was accustomed to seeing while I was growing up in California. My grandparents lived in a city that had a lot of dairy farms. For miles away you could smell manure, and as you got closer, you could see black and white for as far as your eyes could see.

These dairy cattle had a job. They were bred, cared for and milked to supply people with fresh milk in the grocery stores. They were friendly and used to people, and had huge barns where they could get out of the elements if they wanted.

Now, Texas cattle are a whole different story. As far as you can see is pasture lands with black dots lining the horizons. These cattle, while bred and raised for a purpose, spend their lives out on the range. They are born and live out their lives without much human interaction. Very few have large barns where they can retreat into out of the weather, and most are not very acquainted with people.

When we brought the cattle home, they were terrified of us. They did not want anything to do with us aliens that had abducted them into a strange, rolling metal contraption and dropped them off in a new location. When it rained, and let me tell you if it is raining, more than likely, it is a downpour; they didn't retreat to their shelter or barns. They stood out in the elements and even continued on grazing through the rain.

Josephine taught me very quickly that she was not like these big beef cattle. She hated rain! She didn't want to be wet, she didn't want to walk in a puddle, and she surely was not going to be expected to eat outdoors if there was water falling from the sky. She would go to great lengths, and long jumping strides, to avoid getting her precious feet wet.

She would take refuge in her barn, for no matter how long it might take, until the sky stopped crying and the sun came back out.

The first thing God spoke to me about Josephine's hatred of rain was, that like her, we need a covering over our heads; a shelter; a place of refuge from life's storms.

We get this place of refuge, by being involved in our local churches. God's intentions for people have always been unity. When God created man in the garden of Eden, it was for Him to have fellowship with him. When He created Eve, it was for Adam to have fellowship with someone like himself. When God sent Jesus to live as a man, and die for our sins, it was so that we could be reconciled back into fellowship with our Father. The kingdom of God revolves around these relationships with others.

The church is where we are fed from the heart of God, where we have relationships with the body, and where we draw a source of anointing from in our lives. God did not give all of His giftings to one person; each person has a unique set of gifts, and we need each other to build up and help each other through life. Our place of shelter is the covering of a church.

"And let us consider one another in order to stir up love and good works, not forsaking the assembling of ourselves together, as is the manner of some, but exhorting one another, and so much the more as you see the Day approaching."
Hebrews 10:24-25

We cannot afford to forsake assembling together with other believers for church. I hear all the time, "I have Jesus in my heart, I don't need church," or, "We have church by watching so-and-so on tv." I hate to break it to you, but that is not the same thing. Yes, Jesus does live in your heart, and yes, you can be blessed by watching so-and-so on TV. We come together to build the church of Jesus, to draw on one another for strength and help, and to be a blessing to other members of the body of Christ.

I am not saying you cannot meet God where you are at; I am saying you cannot meet His body where you are at, and that is what you are called to do. You will get so much more out of a sermon, by being in a place surrounded by those of like faith, feeling the anointing that goes out as God's word is spoken, and engaging your gifts to lift others up.

In this life, there will be storms. There will come a time that we need a refuge, and that place is a church.

The second thing that God showed me about shelter, is that Josephine has a shepherd that cares for her. I clean barns, bring food and water, patch roofs... well, actually, I don't patch the roofs, my husband does, as I supervise the activity. Josephine has someone to watch over her, to make sure she goes the right direction as she takes steps out of her pasture, or to make sure what she is being fed is correct, or to make sure her feet are trimmed so they are planted firmly on the ground as she walks.

She isn't a lone ranger. She cannot do all of these things by herself, and while I can imagine what a funny sight it would be to see her patch the roof on her barn, it is a sight that is not realistic.

"Obey those who rule over you, and be submissive, for they watch out for your

**souls, as those who must give account. Let them do so with joy and not with grief, for that would be unprofitable for you."
Hebrews 13:17**

We need to be submitted under the authority of our pastors by being a member of a church and by honoring them in word and in action. Pastors are an amazing resource in our lives; if we will let them be.

I am personally submitted under wonderful pastors that truly watch over my soul, speak into my life, and are available to me if I need them. There have been so many times, when I ask for their agreement with me in prayer and they are faithful to do that. I may be my own person, but I still need a shepherd over me to help guide me as I go.

**"But when He (Jesus) saw the multitudes, He was moved with compassion for them, because they were weary and scattered, like sheep having no shepherd. Then He said to His disciples, 'The harvest truly is plentiful, but the laborers are few. Therefore pray the Lord of the harvest to send out laborers into His harvest.'"
Matthew 9:36-38**

Jesus knew the importance of having a

shepherd. He forever remains our Shepherd, but He spoke of the importance of having earthly shepherds to keep us, watch over us and guide us. This goes hand in hand with having a church body. The TV preacher you watch instead of going to church cannot be your pastor. He doesn't know you, you don't have access to him, and he can't watch over your soul from afar. We need to be under a pastor, sitting under his teachings, and to know them in person for them to be able to care for us.

Josephine needed me in person to watch over her. A TV rancher would not have fit the bill; the most successful rancher in the world would not have even worked if she wasn't in his herd and under his direct care.

It is the same way with us; we have to be in a shepherd's fold to be properly fed, cared for and watched over. In times of trouble, who you are submitted to could make or break you. If you have someone who can come along side of you and pray, it makes all the difference in the world. If you think you can go it alone, and that you don't need anyone else, you are in for huge disappointments. A flock isn't a flock with only a member of one.

Above: Josephine before and after

Below: Our original herd

A GOAT NAMED JOSEPHINE

Above: David loving on a kid

Below: David milking in the dairy

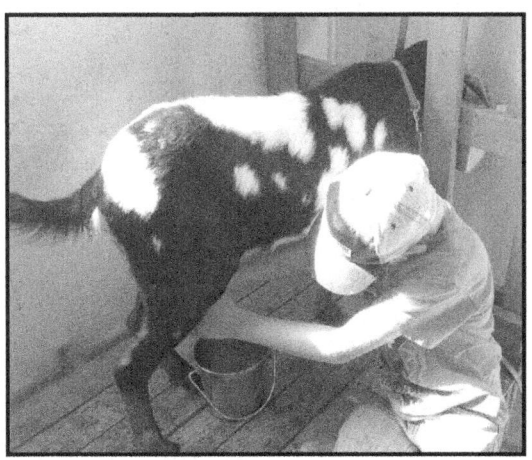

Above: Ryan competing at the Texas State Fair

Below: Safety in Numbers

Above: Ryan & Karisma Lynn

Below: Up close and personal with Flop

5

Pedicures

I have already told you about the poor body condition that Josephine had been in when we brought her home. The lady we bought her from had taken her from someone else that was giving up on her, to let her die; and she had nursed her back to health before we got her. I saw pictures of what Josephine had looked like when this lady saved her, and even though she had already come a long way, she still had a ways to go.

One of the areas that Josephine had really suffered in was her hooves. Goats need their hooves trimmed regularly to keep their toes aligned correctly, which helps their leg bones to be in the correct positions for them to be able to walk correctly. In the grand scheme of things, taking care of hooves seems like a very small thing, but, in reality, if your goat does not have hooves, they don't have feet and if they don't have feet, you don't have a goat.

Josephine's hooves were so overgrown that they actually curled over. Her toes were forced to be out of position causing her to not have a natural, fluid gate and her foot began to turn outward to compensate for the overgrown hooves. With every step, her foot should have been straight in front of her, but instead her foot veered to the side.

As I began the tremendous undertaking of trying to correct her hooves, God began to speak to me about the importance of having your feet in the proper direction.

"Ponder the path of your feet, and let all your ways be established. Do not turn to the right or the left; Remove your foot from evil." Proverbs 4:26-27

God has a plan for each and every one of us; a plan that puts us on a path to accomplish His will for our lives. He doesn't put us on auto-pilot, and we just breeze through this life without having to make decisions, or face challenges, or detours. We will face turns and winding roads and unexpected delays; but keeping on His path is what is vital.

If God has a plan for our lives, then so does the devil. We can walk the straight path of God's plan, or we can veer to the side and stumble onto the other path.

"And if it seems evil to you to serve the LORD, choose for yourselves this day whom you will serve, whether the gods which your fathers served that were on the other side of the River, or the gods of the Amorites, in whose land you dwell. But as for me and my house, we will serve the LORD." Joshua 24:15

Every day, with our words, thoughts, and actions; we choose whom we are serving and what path that will take us down. A little white lie won't hurt anything, right? A slip of a curse word? A replaying of an offense over and over in your mind?

These are all choices that place your foot either on God's path for your day and ultimately your life; or on the path of the world; the path of the devil.

Where you place your feet, determines what path you will follow today.

6

Man Makes Plans...

Half a year had gone by, and Josephine looked amazing. She was shiny and beautiful, her feet were finally fixed, her health was great and she had made our ranch her home. I began to dream about increasing my herd, and as I did so, Josephine was at the center of it all.

I wanted to find someone that had a male dairy goat so that I could have little Josephines running around. If you have never watched a baby goat, called a kid, run around and twist and hop; it is an image that you must see. They are way too cute!

I found someone that my husband worked with that happened to have goats, and we began to talk about having Josephine bred. We talked pricing and when and how and lots of other details, and we decided that I needed to go take a look at her animals and see what I thought.

We set an appointment and I went to her ranch, and quickly learned that this was not a friend that had a couple of goats; this was a goat ranch with all shapes and sizes and breeds. The lady had a dairy business that supplied local exotic farms with milk for their newly born fawns (baby deer) and made cheese and did lots of other things. My head was swimming! What started as a day to meet Josephine's betrothed, turned into a new vision of where this one little goat could lead me.

The owner showed me around and introduced me to lots of her goats. I met her male goat that Josephine would meet in a few months, and I also came home with an unexpected surprise; a new momma and baby goat pair!

My desire for goat milk came to life when these two came to live on our ranch. Suddenly, I had a momma goat in milk that would have to be milked at least once a day! My plan to just find a mate for Josephine, turned into an increase in my herd. I had made plans, but God had ordered my steps.

"A man's heart plans his way, But the LORD directs his steps." Proverbs 16:9

I would have never foreseen this outcome of a trip to someone's farm. I didn't have it planned that way, but God opened a huge door not only for an increase in my herd, but in the joining of a friendship between the ranch owner and myself. She is a lovely Christian woman who continually gives God the glory in all that goes on in her life. She is an encouragement and a blessing to me spiritually, and in my goat life.

7

A Believer Believes

After Bea came to live on our ranch with her kid, and I struggled through learning how to milk her; we had some large learning curves to navigate. When I tried her milk at my new goat friend's ranch, it was so good. It tasted better than cow's milk, with just a touch of sweetness to it. After I had Bea home for a few days, I tasted her milk and it was like taking a bite out of a piece of grass; roots, dirt and all! It was horrible!

I called my friend to ask what had happened, and she began to troubleshoot what I had done wrong, and it all came down to what hay I was feeding her.

I was feeding a good quality grass hay, but it wasn't the correct one! I immediately went to the feed store and brought home the correct grass hay, and after a couple of days, her milk was back to drinkable!

My friend had been telling me a lot about goat milk and about the health benefits of it. She had even said that people who are allergic or intolerant to cow's milk, would be able to drink goat milk. I wasn't sure I believed that, and I began to do some research of my own. (As I am writing this, I realize that I research a lot! Wow!)

Sure enough, it is stated that goat's milk can be consumed by people that cannot ingest cow milk. My mind began to swirl, because I happen to have someone like that in my family and they were coming for a visit very soon.

My mother cannot have cow dairy! It hurts her stomach, it messes with her joints and creates a lot of pain throughout her body. Even a trace amount gives her horrific side effects, and for most of my life, I have watched her suffer even when the very last ingredient in something is a dairy derivative. Her intolerance is severe!

When she came to the ranch, she was so excited to meet our new little herd. Growing up, she had been raised with livestock and had milk cows, and she was so ready to dive in and milk. She, and I, quickly learned that milking a cow and milking a goat are very different. I could milk, and she struggled. We laughed and squirted everything but the pail, and worked on getting her form right. By a couple of sessions, she was a milking pro.

Getting the milk proved a challenge, but the real question was, could she drink it?

When my mom is here, some of my favorite times with her is in the mornings as the sun comes up and we sit and drink our coffee and talk or read our Bibles. I love those moments with her, they are priceless. The next morning after she arrived, we began to make our coffees and she decided she was going to take the plunge and try goat milk in her coffee. I held my breath, and waited for symptoms to appear.

I felt like those shipwrecked men in the Bible, on an island with Paul after he had gotten bitten by a viper, watching him and expecting him to start showing symptoms and die.

"But when Paul had gathered a bundle of sticks and laid them on the fire, a viper came out because of the heat, and fastened on his hand. So when the natives saw the creature hanging from his hand, they said to one another, 'No doubt this man is a murderer, whom, though he has escaped the sea, yet justice does not allow to live.' But he shook off the creature into the fire and suffered no harm. However, they were expecting that he would swell up or suddenly fall down dead. But after they had looked for a long time and saw no harm come to him, they changed their minds and said that he was a god." Acts 28:3-6

Five minutes in and no symptoms. Ten minutes. No symptoms. I could not believe that I had just seen my mother drink milk and she had absolutely no side effects! From that first sip on, she was not only sold on goat milk, but she was hooked! She made breakfast gravy, pancakes and biscuits all with goat milk and she lived! Seriously, we all could not believe it! We were all sold on goat's milk and visions of a full scale dairy began to take hold in our thoughts.

We made cheese, we ate and drank milk and we even made a couple batches of soap while she was here. I had two adult goats but only one had milk and I began to think I needed more goats.

As my Mom prepared to leave, we packed her a cooler with cheese and milk and all of the glorious things that this goat milk had provided. We had a serious discussion about getting more goats and maybe making a room in one of our barns into a dairy. A seed had been planted in both of us!

I took it to God. I knew I wanted more milk and more goats, and I began to think of the time when I could finally have Josephine bred so that those things could be accomplished. I again began to make mental plans, but God had another direction.

Within a month, my goat friend called with an opportunity to purchase 2 momma and kid pairs, and we jumped on the opportunity. We doubled our herd in a day and went from half a gallon every day to 2 gallons every day, and man my hands were getting a work out! It was more than I could have dreamed of, or hoped for.

Emma Byers

"You shall have enough goats' milk for your food, for the food of your household, And the nourishment of your maidservants." Proverbs 27:27

8

Isolation

We had a herd of eight goats, more than we ever dreamed we would have, but not beyond what our new vision for our herd was. The girls had all settled in with each other and into their new barn and things were going well. It was mid-summer and we were quickly approaching the time when I would finally get to have Josephine bred. I had picked out the perfect male to compliment her, and was anticipating the time when my dream from the day I brought Josephine home, would come to pass.

I had gone out to feed and noticed that Josephine did not come to the gate like she always did. She stood back away from the herd, backed into a corner all by herself. As I fed everyone else, she came out and nibbled at the grain and I scratched her and looked her over, and she seemed ok, just a bit off. I decided to keep an eye on her, and by the next morning her demeanor had not changed.

The first sign in a goat that there may be something up is a fever, so I took her temperature, and sure enough she was running a very high fever. I started her on heavy antibiotics, probiotics, vitamin b injections, and prayed over her. We gave her electrolytes throughout the day and by the next day, she was down on the ground, and didn't want to get up. We continued treatment and prayers, and I noticed that the only time she would get up was if her other herd members would come around her. She didn't want to be with them, she wanted to be alone; isolated, away from everyone else.

I realized that she knew something was not right and she separated herself away from everyone. Goats are a herd animal, they thrive in a herd, and here she was putting distance between herself and them.

Many times when we have things going on in our lives, we too draw ourselves back from the people we love, or from our church, or put walls up between us and the world. Many times it is from emotional distress, or from the condemnation of a sin that we allowed in our lives, or other reasons.

The Bible says that we are one body, that we are to aid each other, to help one another in times of need, to lift up each other when we lack the strength to do so ourselves. Whether we like it or not, we need people to help us, and they need us to help them.

"But now God has set the members, each one of them, in the body just as He pleased. And if they were all one member, where would the body be? But now indeed there are many members, yet one body. And the eye cannot say to the hand, "I have no need of you"; nor again the head to the feet, "I have no need of you." No, much rather, those members of the body which seem to be weaker are necessary. And those members of the body which we think to be

less honorable, on these we bestow greater honor; and our unpresentable parts have greater modesty, but our presentable parts have no need. But God composed the body, having given greater honor to that part which lacks it, that there should be no schism in the body, but that the members should have the same care for one another. And if one member suffers, all the members suffer with it; or if one member is honored, all the members rejoice with it." 1 Corinthians 12:18-26

In a herd, there is safety in numbers. If a predator should ever come, he will set his sights on the animal that is away from the herd. He looks for opportunities to separate an individual member out, and then moves in for the kill. The animals that are tightly bound in the herd, are protected.

There is a type of goat called a Myotonic Goat, or the common name is a Fainting Goat. If you have never witnessed a fainting goat in action, you should look it up on the internet, because I promise you, the videos are hilarious! A fainting goat does what its name implies; when it is frightened, it faints. Now while this is funny to witness, it is also where the term "scape goat" comes in.

To protect valuable herds, shepherds have fainting goats mixed in with their other animals. When a predator comes after the herd and they all take flight out of fear, the fainting goat doesn't run; he faints. He lays down in the midst of fear, and the predator preys upon him instead of chasing down the rest of the herd.

You don't want to be a fainting goat! There are two important lessons from fainting goats. The first thing is, do not be the isolated one; and the second thing is, you cannot allow fear to paralyze you and expect to survive the enemy.

We have an enemy, and **John 10:10** tells us,

"The thief does not come except to steal, and to kill, and to destroy."

He doesn't come to hang out and see what you're up to. He doesn't come to tempt you with some "fun." He comes to steal, kill and destroy. Notice it doesn't say, "He comes to steal or to kill or to destroy?" When the devil comes after you, he comes to steal and to kill and to destroy.

The devil is on the prowl. If you're a Christian, you are on his radar, and he is looking for an opportunity to attack you.

'Be sober, be vigilant; because your adversary the devil walks about like a roaring lion, seeking whom he may devour.'
1 Peter 5:8

That is a solemn thought, that you can either allow to paralyze you, or empower you with faith. If you go paralyzed, well my friend, you have just become a fainting goat; but if you rise up and stand your ground on the word of God and combat the devil, then you will be victorious.

If you have wandered from your herd, make things right, change your heart and get back within the safety of numbers. Come back under the Shepherd's care and abide in safety and peace. Don't be a sick goat, isolated off from everyone, that becomes an easy target for any enemy that is on the prowl.

After a few days of Josephine being so sick, she started to get up and eat and even tried to rejoin the herd. I was so excited that she was on the mend, and we continued to treat her. Usually if goats get sick, they die very quickly and now that we had been going through this for almost a week and she seemed to be getting better, I could finally breathe a sigh of relief. She spent her days up and eating, coming to the gate and began to act like her old self. I continued to monitor and take temperatures and give vitamins and electrolytes and we seemed like we had turned the corner.

The next morning, as I headed to the pen, I could see something white on the ground, and my heart sank. I knew my beautiful Josephine had a white belly, and I was pretty sure that she was on the ground again. As I got closer, I realized, she wasn't down, she had passed away. I broke down into sobbing tears, crying out to God.

I had named her and declared over her, and when she fell sick, I prayed and believed and did everything I knew to do, and then some; and yet I still lost her. I didn't understand. I was so heartbroken. All those months of planning and dreaming of the herd that would come from her, slipped right through my fingers. I knelt down next to her and ran my hands through the coat that I had worked so hard to make beautiful and healthy and just asked God to help. I didn't even know what to ask of Him, other than to help me understand. We came so far, to lose so much.

It was in the midst of my broken heart that God spoke to me and said, "Look around, see your increase."

Increase? I never got to breed her! She never had kids! The herd I envisioned her bringing forth never came to be, and now it never would. It was almost a laughable thought, and I brushed it out of my mind as I laid my Josephine to rest.

When the sun rose the next morning and I headed solemnly out to the barns to feed, grief hung over my heart. I still couldn't make sense of the whole thing. She had been getting better! I had named her a name that declared that God would increase every time that her name passed over my lips! I knew that God's word never returns void, and I just felt so shaken and frustrated

"So shall My word be that goes forth from My mouth; It shall not return to Me void, But it shall accomplish what I please, And it shall prosper in the thing for which I sent it." Isaiah 55:1

As my girls met me at the gate, truth hit me like a sack of rocks to the gut. God had increased!

He took one lowly, malnourished goat and turned it into a herd, a vision, and a passion. Where I saw one goat, He provided seven more. Where I had seen milk in my refrigerator, He supplied enough for soap and cheese. Where I had seen a hobby, he brought a passion to me and my children.

When Josephine came here, I never dreamed that I would make soap or cheese or that this would turn into a herd that produces show kids for my boys to compete with. My vision was so small, but God had big plans. Now, I do not believe that it was God's plan for Josephine to get sick, or to pass away. My God doesn't work that way! He brings life abundant; and sickness, disease and death are not abundant life. But, when things happen in this fallen world, there will be something good that will come from it.

9

My Way or His Way?

I had a vision, a way that I was sure that my herd would go. I had dreamt about it, prayed about it, declared over it; and yet, I had lost the goat at the center of my dreams. My vision was very literally dead. Now what?

Many times we are faced with a situation that takes us to our knees, seeking the very face of God, interceding in prayer and believing for a miracle until that miracle comes to pass. But what happens when it doesn't? Where do you go when the pieces cannot be put back together.

In that moment you have the opportunity to question God and if He really hears your prayers, or you can tighten your boot straps, stand fast in your faith and know that in this fallen world things do not always work out like we think they should.

"And we know that all things work together for good to those who love God, to those who are the called according to His purpose." Romans 8:28

While God knew that I would lose Josephine, it was never His plan to bring death and hurt into my life. The Bible tells us that,

"Every good gift and every perfect gift is from above, and comes down from the Father of lights, with whom there is no variation or shadow of turning." James 1:17

His plan was to bless the work of my hands and to fulfill the desires of my heart. His plan was to teach me things about Himself through one sickly goat. His plan was to bring increase and a new vision, when my vision would come to an end.

God had brought increase. Albeit, it wasn't how I thought it would happen, but nonetheless, increase had come. I have an amazing herd, with bloodlines that I could never have known to desire, and goats that were supernaturally brought across my path.

Yes, I did suffer a loss close to my heart, and yes it hurt; but God had a plan to redeem what the devil had stolen.

"So I will restore to you the years that the swarming locust has eaten, The crawling locust, The consuming locust, And the chewing locust, My great army which I sent among you. You shall eat in plenty and be satisfied, And praise the name of the LORD your God, Who has dealt wondrously with you; And My people shall never be put to shame. Then you shall know that I am in the midst of Israel: I am the LORD your God And there is no other. My people shall never be put to shame." Joel 2:25-27

I know that there is someone reading this that has suffered a loss, been hurt or is wondering why God didn't step in to a situation they prayed for.

Let me reassure you,

God has never left you.

In the midst of loss, disappointment, disaster, heartache, brokenness, or despair; God is with you, holding your broken heart, trying to restore you back to completion. You don't have to look too hard, or too far, to feel His loving arms around you, to hear His still small voice, and to know that He is still working on your behalf.

"He heals the brokenhearted And binds up their wounds." Psalm 147:3

God is ready, willing and able to take your brokenness and bring wholeness to it. He is ready to take your mess and give you a message; your test and give you a testimony; your defeat and give you victory.

A NOTE FROM THE AUTHOR

When God began to speak to me about writing this book, I was hurting, my goat was dead, I felt defeat all around and I couldn't imagine anyone reading a book where the main character dies. I am going to be honest, I laughed, and then cried; argued, and then tried to reason; and in the end this is what He told me,

"In My book, My only Son died, and people have been changed all over the world for thousands of years."

I wrote out of obedience, and I believe that the words that God has given me to put on paper, will bring blessings, encouragement, help, and words of promise and life into each person who reads it.

If you don't get anything else from this book, I want you to know that *JESUS LOVES YOU*. He gave His life for you. He has called you and has a plan for your life. You are a cherished child of the King.

"For God so loved the world that He gave His only begotten Son, that whoever believes in Him should not perish but have everlasting life. For God did not send His Son into the world to condemn the world, but that the world through Him might be saved." John 3:16-17

Emma Byers

Look for these other titles by Emma Byers:

The Lies the Devil Told Me

Ingrafted: A 52 Week Devotional

Coming in 2017:

Lessons From the Barnyard vol. 2

Made in the USA
Columbia, SC
05 July 2022